Flip the Script

Published by 404 Ink Limited
www.404Ink.com
@404Ink

Editing: Heather McDaid
Typesetting: Laura Jones
Cover design: Luke Bird
Co-founders and publishers of 404 Ink: Heather McDaid & Laura Jones

Print ISBN: 978-1-912489-30-5
Ebook ISBN: 978-1-912489-31-2

Printed and bound in Great Britain by Clays Ltd, Elcograf S.p.A.

404 Ink acknowledges support for this title from
Creative Scotland via the Crowdmatch initiative.

Flip the Script

How Women Came to Rule Hip Hop

Arusa Qureshi

Inklings

For Lucy Munro;
an amazing woman, dearly missed.

Contents

Playlist

If you're looking for the perfect soundtrack to the book, you can listen to Arusa's 'Flip the Script' playlist over on Spotify by searching 'Flip the Script: Women and Hip Hop', or by using the QR code below.

It can also be found at 404ink.com/flipthescript.

Enjoy.

Introduction:
Bad bitch alert

Hip hop is an art form that originated in the margins, and can be simultaneously devastating and celebratory; an expression of pain, love and desire or an ode to the other, the underdog and the underground. It is empowerment and subversion, but also full of contradictions and unresolved controversy. It's all of these things and much more. For me though, it's the crucial association with social movements, revolutionary campaigns and cultural awareness, as well as protest and activism, that proves that hip hop can be a safe haven, especially for the oppressed.

Hip hop has always been something of a safe haven for me. Many would likely consider this an unusual statement to make, with a phrase like 'safe haven' perhaps viewed as the antithesis to hip hop, but creatively,

1

mentally and emotionally, it has been the place that I've landed throughout my adult life when my mind is in desperate need of a boost. My own connection to hip hop was forged in the '90s and early '00s, where I grew up with a music taste largely defined by an older sister who gravitated towards R&B and hip hop as a teenager. I remember vividly dancing around our living room while MTV blasted out music videos by the likes of TLC, Biggie and Aaliyah – just a few of our favourites. One of my earliest memories of my little brother also strangely revolves around the genre. Struggling to sleep as a newborn, we soon discovered that he had a natural fascination with the aforementioned music videos. So, my sister taped a random selection that were on heavy rotation, including 2Pac's 'Changes', Missy Elliott's 'Get Ur Freak On' and OutKast's 'Ms. Jackson', and my brother would be gently rocked to sleep against the soothing backdrop of gangsta rap and alternative hip hop. This unorthodox method would have him snoring away in less than fifteen minutes and so began the legacy of 'The Tape'. Why my fairly traditional, Muslim, South Asian mother encouraged this, I'll never fully under-stand. But I think she secretly really liked Missy Elliott.

We were the type of first generation immigrant kids that naturally rebelled against our parents' desire to assimilate into their South Asian heritage and so we looked to music and TV instead for a different cultural fix. We brushed off Bollywood in favour of American hip hop and shunned our parents' Asian sitcoms and soaps for *The Fresh Prince of Bel Air* and *Sister Sister*. Black American culture spoke to us and, growing up in Scotland with very few brown people around, it was our only immediate bridge to other people of colour. Sure, it wasn't our culture and it wasn't about our experiences, but there was something in hip hop in particular that made me feel like it was okay to be the only brown person in the room.

My own teens were dominated by an all-consuming love for Nirvana and everything grunge but in the background, hip hop was always there. When I was around fifteen, I started writing, mostly silly poems and rambling essays about music, but I was also obsessed with pulling apart lyrics, trying to really understand what was being said and why. The Golden Age of hip hop was where I found most comfort at this point; the stylistic innovations, eclectic cadences and fast rhymes of the era drawing me in like no other form. This deep-seated interest never left me, only intensifying as I learnt more about the originators and pioneers of the genre, as well as what was happening in the present, in contemporary hip hop.

It all reached a climax at university. I took my interest a step further and wrote my undergraduate dissertation on the form. Studying English Literature, hip hop came up in exactly one slide in one lecture on vernacular poetry, but that was all the permission I needed. Sadly, my supervisor didn't see it that way. He encouraged me to switch topics, commenting, "I don't understand the point of hip hop. I don't mind Jay-Z too much though…"

There were no people of colour on the department's teaching staff and I felt as if I wasn't taken seriously with my 'lofty' hip hop academia. Being determined (and desperate to stick it to the old white man who dismissed me), I went for it anyway. The topic? Defiance in hip hop. I've never felt as passionate about researching and writing something as I did that dissertation, and it sparked a lifelong dream to write about music professionally and academically. Which leads me quite nicely to the title of this introduction: Bad Bitch Alert.

In 2015, I was commissioned to write my first article for The List magazine. The article 'Bad Bitch Alert' was my take on how female MCs – including Lizzo and Leikeli47 – were challenging hip hop's male reign. Women have occupied a vital space in hip hop from its very beginnings in the Bronx in the '70s but men have always dominated in one way or another, with gendered hierarchies becoming ingrained in the genre itself. I was lucky in that I was exposed to everyone from Salt-N-Pepa and Left Eye to Queen Latifah and Missy Elliott early on thanks to my older sister. Women were very much a big part of everything I knew about hip hop and, in many ways, the reason I started falling for hip hop in the first place. Seeing not only people of colour but women of colour on screen – powerful, confident and completely in control – contributed to what I believed was possible for us growing up. It contributed to my idea of this safe haven. It was obvious, though, in terms of the videos that were being played on loop on MTV and the rappers that were climbing the charts who was ruling the roost. I didn't care though. Before I knew anything about misogyny or stereotypes, hip hop was female empowerment epitomised.

When I came to write that article, armed with years of research and analysis on the precarious relationship between women and hip hop over the past few decades, I really did believe that something was changing in the pecking order. I still do, all these years later. But crucially, it's not just changing where it all began in the US.

Despite being the geographical focus of *Flip the Script*, the UK hasn't made a significant appearance yet – there's a reason for that. Since my childhood was so heavily governed by American pop culture, I didn't listen to or really know what was happening in the UK scene. It wasn't until I reached my late teens that I started to properly appreciate the sheer strength and vivacity of UK hip hop and its various iterations. People like Roots Manuva, Klashnekoff and Ms. Dynamite were just some of the artists rightfully taking up space in my music collection and playlists, but it took some time. When I was finally able to go back and delve a bit deeper into how the country adopted this Black American art form, I realised that it wasn't just a case of adoption, it was the creation and restyling of a genre that spoke to an audience with a very specific social and political history. Many early UK rappers attempted to mimic the American sound, down to the accent, because it was popular and could potentially lead to commercial success. There were others, like the formidable London Posse, who took this genre of music from the Bronx and transplanted it into a very distinct and localised context, speaking for a generation of Black Brits born and raised in the UK. The descendants of the Windrush Generation and their part in sound system culture played a key role in the formation of UK hip hop, giving it a unique and authentic narrative that reflected the socio-political landscape, while still engaging with core themes found in its American roots like racism, violence, poverty and justice.

What always strikes me is how few women are included in any historical analysis of the genre or 'best of all-time' lists in the UK when, just like in the US, women have been in attendance since day one. It's not about women not existing; it's about visibility and often erasure. If hip hop is a vital cultural force and haven for the oppressed, how are the voices of many core figures so easily forgotten?

As I've continued towards my goals of hip hop scholarship, I've increasingly felt drawn to celebrating these voices and the genre keeps giving me all the more reason to. The unbelievable level of skill and finesse we're currently seeing bubbling up in UK hip hop, especially from women, only accelerated in a year marked by lockdowns, cancellations and postponements. The winners of both the Scottish Album of the Year Award and the Welsh Music Prize in 2020 were female rappers, Nova and Deyah respectively. It indicated a seismic shift in both the music industry's mentality towards women – with emphasis on women of colour – and the general public's approach to hip hop as a respected and valued art form. More, it hinted at how UK hip hop cannot and should not be viewed exclusively through the lens of its capital city. Hip hop can be that bridge for many people to other cultures, as it was for me growing up in Scotland. Within these regional scenes, women are not only thriving, but importantly, dominating and leading the charge.

When I wrote that Bad Bitch Alert article, Nicki Minaj had already been nominated for seven Grammy Awards. Soon, Cardi B would release her first full-length project and Megan Thee Stallion was close behind with her debut single. It was a good time commercially for women in hip hop and this has snowballed since. This is where I feel we are with hip hop in the UK – at the cusp of something incredible. It's time to embrace the changing of the guard.

Flip the Script is a homage to the women who are innovating and revitalising the genre, the future MCs and leaders of hip hop and those that were there at the very beginning. The list of names that deserve credit is limitless, but this is a celebration of what we have to look forward to, a snapshot of that musical magic... This is me welcoming you to my safe haven. May it become yours too.

Chapter 1:

The women who built the scene

When considering the history of women in hip hop, there are some names that will always stand out. There's Debbie D, a member of DJ Marley Marl's Juice Crew; Pebblee Poo, who joined DJ Kool Herc's Herculoids; and Lisa Lee, who was in Afrika Bambaataa's Universal Zulu Nation. Then, of course, there's Sha-Rock, considered the first prominent female MC, and Mercedes Ladies, the first all-female group in hip hop. These names are a fundamental piece of the wider hip hop puzzle while simultaneously being relegated to the footnotes of history. Without these women, the genre would be nowhere near as rich, bold and full of fire as it is today. These women were the pioneers.

There's a notorious story in the culture's canon – that of Roxanne Shanté. Native to Queens, New York, she began rapping as a child, quickly becoming a central figure in the scene at just 14 thanks to her battle rap track 'Roxanne's Revenge'. Written in response to UTFO's 'Roxanne, Roxanne', it was a song about a fictional woman that kept brushing off the male group's advances. In her daring and confrontational response, Shanté embodied this fictional character, creating an instant hit and inspiring a whole generation of diss tracks in the process. She wasn't a one-hit wonder or a mere marketing pawn, she had undeniable skills as an MC and battle rapper; as a young woman she was considered a threat to many men in the scene. It was at the annual MC Battle for World Supremacy in 1985 where this came to a head.

The competition, known for creating legends and spotlighting the best MCs in the game, was the setting for an event that dimmed Shanté's light. The only woman competing, she made the final against Busy Bee Starski. Despite being the better rapper and clear favourite, she was defeated in what can only be described as a fix, ending with her in tears. Listening back to the audio from the battle, which exists on YouTube, Shanté dominates; the cheers alone as she rolls out diss after diss confirm this. Starski does well, but pales in comparison as Shanté gradually gets increasingly riled up, energy never faltering. She delivers the kind of verbal take-down that makes you proud of her, all these years later.

In her excellent illustrated anthology *The Motherlode*, writer Clover Hope details the battle and judge Kurtis Blow purposely giving Shanté a low score because "he didn't like the optics of a girl winning a rap battle, no matter how much she outperformed her opponent."[1] It's fairly well established, even by Blow himself, that Shanté did in fact win. In Kathy Iandoli's *God Save the Queens*, she notes how many viewed Blow's actions that day as his attempt to prevent women from leading the next phase of hip hop. Iandoli quotes Busy Bee, who told her, "I think they weren't ready for a female to take the helm", later herself asking, "So what would've happened if that new guard had been led by a woman?"[2]

The events of that battle always stuck with me as a significant moment in early hip hop that marked its future. Not only because Shanté came closer to dethroning her male counterparts than anyone before but also because it is widely acknowledged Shanté should have won. She was the best rapper there but in the words of Clover Hope, "Everyone told her she was nice for a girl."[3] In all facets of the music industry, women have been told similar; they're good *for a girl*, they make decent music *for a girl*. It is perhaps one of the core reasons women are left out of the history of the genres they revolutionise.

That same year, in the UK, another competition was taking place. Two young women from Clapham, south London were about to storm a national rap championship at The Wag Club which would launch their entire career. They would quickly go on to capture the attention of the UK hip hop scene as well as key industry figures like John Peel. But two years earlier in 1983, MC Remedee (Debbie Pryce) and Susie Q (Susan Banfield) were just getting started as Cookie Crew, inspired by what was happening in the New York music scene. Cookie Crew pre-dated other prominent women in UK hip hop like She Rockers and Wee Papa Girl Rappers, not to mention Monie Love, who would go on to settle in New York in 1988 to massive success. As one of the first female hip hop groups in the UK, they were also among the first to battle the hurdles women faced in the genre; constantly compared to adjacent male rappers, forced to prove themselves despite their evident success, and constantly pushed in different, and often contradictory, directions.

"We started listening to hip hop because Debbie would go to New York with her family in the early '80s, record the radio on a cassette tape and bring it back for us to listen to," Susie explains. "We would listen to it at home, and it was amazing to us. We started to hear different styles of rap on these cassette tapes that were basically New York radio and we said to each other, we could do that so let's try and write something."

The pair would spend time in the park near where they grew up with their crew of friends, roller skating and playing double dutch – once they started writing, this was the ideal place to test the waters with their rhymes. Around the same time, the BBC broadcast a documentary called *Beat This: A Hip Hop History*, which caught the attention of the young rappers-to-be. In the documentary, Malcolm McLaren – best known for his contributions to punk rock via managing the Sex Pistols – talks about his introduction to Afrika Bambaataa's Zulu Nation in the south Bronx.

"Malcolm McLaren did this documentary in a place in Covent Garden where breakers used to hang out," Susie recalls. "We started to connect the dots with everything that was happening in the hip hop scene. There were graffiti artists down there, there were breakers, and there were rappers – everyone started to try a little something." This included Susie and Debbie, who were writing raps, not realising that there weren't really other girls doing the same thing locally. "We had no clue because we saw American girls doing it. We were listening to female rappers like Sha-Rock, Lisa Lee and Debbie D and we were influenced by them. There were a lot of rappers out there at the time, all male, but we did see Michelle Devitt also known as Mystery MC of Family Quest. We saw her rapping on stage; she was freestyling and she blew us away – she was the first

13

female rapper that we had seen from England. I didn't see any others before her."

Before long, they were accepted into the fold as rappers in their own right, respected for their rhymes. It was at this point in 1985 that they heard about a rap competition being run by a young Tim Westwood, with prize money and a recording contract up for grabs.

"We heard about it, we thought about it, and the boys that we used to hang with were saying 'You could win this!' And so our friends forced us to go down there, and we put our name down for the first week. We saw all the rappers that were taking part and then thought, *Okay, we'll go back next weekend and take our name off the list, because this is looking really hard and we're not sure.* But the night came and we thought, *We're just gonna go out there and do it because it doesn't matter.* I remember the stage being so big that they had to lift Debbie up onto it! We rapped over Afrika Bambaataa and the Soul Sonic Force's 'Planet Rock', and it was fast. It was so fast!"

"Basically, we killed it," Debbie adds with a grin. "It was a blur as well because the stage felt like a platform so we could see everybody. We could see all the guys from Battersea who came with us, who were our support network. The crowd was just going crazy. They were cheering throughout the whole performance. It ended and we were buzzing. When they made the announcement on the night that we won, it was like our feet didn't touch the ground. It was a complete blur, but it was sheer excitement. We went away feeling like champions and after that, the world was our lobster."

A direct contrast to Shanté's experience, the duo became the names to watch on the scene. They took the prize money but not the contract. "We weren't interested in the recording contract and [it's] a good job we didn't take it because thinking back it probably would have been a mess," Debbie notes. "We went for a meeting and I just remember getting on a tube, going somewhere, having the meeting and coming out unsure. We knew nothing about the business. We just wanted to hang out and build our reputation on the scene. Thank God we didn't sign whatever that contract was – but we did get a trophy!"

That was just the start for Cookie Crew. "It gave us the opportunity to really soak it up, because we were obsessed with hip hop culture," Susie explains. "Hip hop culture to us was graffiti, breaking, DJing, rapping, body popping – those were the elements. There was a whole culture around Covent Garden [the nucleus of London's hip hop scene], which embodied everything about hip hop from the way we dressed to the way we spoke."

Even though this clear identity was being forged in London, the influence of American hip hop was prevalent and crucial to kickstarting the movement.

Cookie Crew were asked to do a show with Afrika Bambaataa, who was touring with DJ Red Alert and Lisa

Lee, someone that Susie and Debbie looked up to from the start. "We got to be on that show with other people from Covent Garden. That to me, out of everything we've done – and we've performed at Wembley, we've supported Bobby Brown, we've lived in New York, we've worked with many different rappers – doing that show, and Lisa Lee being in the audience, was the most nerve-wracking thing I think I've ever, ever done," recalls Susie. "We did a rehearsal where she was sitting in the auditorium watching us and she told us off for one, looking nervous; two, standing still; and three, not giving it enough. So, we went away really annoyed with ourselves, went home, practiced, came back, and came back correct."

In 1987, Cookie Crew had an unexpected hit with 'Rok Da House', created by production team Beatmasters, who they were partnered with at the recommendation of Tim Westwood. While it led to the duo signing with London Records and going international, it's part of their history that they have more complicated feelings about.

"'Rok Da House' was kind of like an accident," Debbie explains. "Beatmasters put together this backing track, we went away and wrote a rap to it. The track had more of a hip hop base but after they mixed it and they played with it, it somehow turned into this house sounding track."

"I think they started playing it in the clubs," Susie ponders. "You know, we were very adamant for them to not associate us with the track. They had ownership of it and we said, *Whatever you want to do with it, it's yours. It's not ours.*"

After having some success on the dancefloors of London, the track made its way to Mark Moore from S'Express. He took it to Rhythm King Records, they loved it, and from there their career took off in new and unexpected ways.

"It just escalated and escalated," Debbie says. "Somehow the record was put out, it started to grow in the clubs again then it got into the charts. Radio One used to do the chart run down every week and they'd phone up the artists live and have a conversation and talk about the record. We went live on air and basically said, *We don't like the record, it's not us.* We were honest. We were young and we were honest. But the record still did its thing and it became this track that we just couldn't get rid of."

Susie remembers how newspapers would call her family home to ask why they didn't want to perform the track and her dad would answer the phone, quite rightly, confused. The duo were adamant about staying true to themselves and their hip hop roots. "We never ever even performed 'Rok Da House' in the end, did we, Debs?"

"We tried to perform it once during a sold out set when the promoter came stomping up to our managers wanting us to play it," Debbie answers. "We attempted it and when we tried it, we were laughing so much that we just couldn't get through the song. He wasn't too happy. It's not a record that we are proud of but I am grateful for it. Looking back, we could have probably dealt with it a bit more strategically, but we were just a couple of girls from south London – we loved hip hop."

After signing with London Records, Cookie Crew took on the USA. It became their home away from home and soon they were ingrained in the US market, working with the likes of Stetsasonic and Gangstarr. But through all of this, they stuck to their truth, and to their British identity, and did all they could to represent the burgeoning scene at home. All three singles from their debut album *Born This Way*, which featured on the UK Albums Chart, make direct reference to their hometown and to their journey. 'Born This Way (Let's Dance)' in particular is an unapologetic overview of who Cookie Crew are and what the duo stand for ("Okay, we're not here to play, no fuzz, no drugs," they say at the start of the music video), snapping back at anyone that ever doubted them ("We've got a message to all who said we couldn't do it, take a look at us now, take your words and chew it," they continue). 'Black Is The Word', another album track, captures the pride in their Black British identity, where 'From The South' is a homage to their home – "going out to all the south London MCs".

"We've always stayed true to our roots because we were very patriotic about London, and about south London, particularly," Debbie says. "All the narratives on the tracks are based around our experiences, even though the delivery might have had that American tone, because that was our reference point. Our subject matters were very, very British. When we were in New York, we were very proud of being British. We also felt that we were educating them about what was going on outside of the US. A lot of the people we met didn't realise that there were actually Black people in England because not many people had passports back then and they weren't travelling. We were educating them on who we were, being British, but British Caribbean too."

Cookie Crew carried a piece of London with them and introduced the growing UK hip hop scene to international contemporaries, emphasising that the UK wasn't just a place for American artists to tour but a country of its own unique hip hop identity.

"We've always been interested and passionate about our own culture, and about our own people, and our journey," Susie explains. "Our references came from our parents, and our parents were the Windrush era. Hip hop in a way introduced us to what was happening in

America but it didn't introduce us to wider issues we faced as Black people. For example, we spent a lot of our time doing anti-apartheid gigs. We spent a lot of time making sure that we were involved with any gig to do with freeing Nelson Mandela as much as we could. We boycotted certain things, we were involved in everything possible that could be against Margaret Thatcher. We've always had that side of us."

The music industry in the US wasn't exactly supportive of such serious messaging, especially in music by women, so they had to have more of a light touch in speaking out publicly. In their next album *Fade to Black*, tracks like 'The Powers of Positive Thinking' and 'A Word to the Conscious' laid bare their thoughts and feelings on vital issues of the day, including the incarceration of Nelson Mandela, the causes of racism and oppression, and gun control.

"Those kind of tracks wouldn't have been chosen as singles – we did them to satisfy us," Debbie says. "We want to make sure that we are able to put into our own content what we feel so that our fans and media could see that there was a serious side to us."

At home, focus had always been on lyrical dexterity and flow but in the US, image was overtaking in terms of importance. The American music industry celebrated Cookie Crew to begin with, but intentions soon went beyond their talent when the pair were encouraged to change their look to fit the mould of others. "Whenever they tried to talk to us about songs," notes Susie, "I think they respected what we were trying to do but deep down, they wanted us to be something else. We didn't come from that; we came from a very tomboyish image and so for us to try and be like Salt-N-Pepa, it wasn't going to work and I think that it was our demise in the end. At that time, when we were going through that weird stage, female rappers were getting more and more sexual. And we were going more and more the other way – we could never compete with that."

"And we weren't willing to compromise," Debbie adds. "We had nothing against them because, you know, we loved Lil' Kim and we loved Salt-N-Pepa. But we couldn't compete. That wasn't our way."

"Female rappers are all about the lyrics and delivering and showing that they are better than the guys," says Susie, on the UK scene. "We felt like that when we first started in 1985, our whole point was to be better than the boys. Because they were the ones that were popular. Why were they more popular than us? We weren't about to go and pimp ourselves out and show a bit of cleavage on stage; we wanted to show lyrically that we could stand next to you and hold our own. I think that female rappers in the UK still have that same mentality and it's definitely a British thing of: *Forget about what you're seeing here, listen to what's coming out of my mouth first.*"

Hip hop has come a long way since the days of Cookie Crew, but without acknowledging those that came first, that battled the barriers of misogyny decades ago – like Shanté's cautionary tale, or Susie and Debbie's experience with the fickle nature of the music industry – we cannot properly appreciate the history of the form and how the way has been paved. While other names like She Rockers and Wee Papa Girl Rappers have their own story and legacy that adds another vital brick in the genre's journey in the UK, Cookie Crew are noteworthy not only for being the first UK women in hip hop to achieve international plaudits, but also for setting the tone for a certain type of consciousness in their rhymes. This sense of activism through poetry and radical thinking was already common in wider hip hop, but the addition of feminist themes like equality, liberation and sisterhood was still relatively new for the UK when Cookie Crew began making their mark.

As we end our conversation, I ask Debbie and Susie what it would be like if Cookie Crew were operating today. They both laugh, remarking that it would be easy to get something out there but the hard part would be them actually getting round to doing it. Hip hop is in a healthy place, both agree, and the women in the scene in particular are doing them and other pioneers proud. "It's just free, it looks good and it's authentic," Susie says, on today's landscape. "That's what I like about it – I see it just getting better and better."

Chapter 2:

The women who spread the word

Hip hop spread like wildfire in the US following The Sugarhill Gang's 'Rapper's Delight' in 1979; it wasn't long before the UK followed suit in its fascination with this bold new art form. Every facet, from graffiti to breakdancing, was eventually welcomed, mainly adopted by inner city Black youth as a means of expression. "Hip Hop was transformed from a 'borrowed culture'," begins writer and academic Andy Wood, "to an identifiably black British form that dealt with specific issues pertinent to a generation of black youths born and brought up in Britain, while also retaining an international outlook and perspective."[1] Alongside Cookie Crew, groups and artists like Family Quest,

Demon Boyz, Outlaw Posse, Derek B, Cash Crew and London Posse soon dominated the field by making it their own, speaking on themes and issues that were relevant to young people in the UK at that time. London Posse's tongue-in-cheek self-titled debut single touched on the group's experiences in the US, where they caused intrigue with their mixture of Cockney and Jamaican accents, even incorporating the tune of 'London Bridge is Falling Down' in the song when talking about "getting high" and meeting American "birds". Meanwhile, Cash Crew's classic 1990 single 'Green Grass' was all about global warming, almost prescient with references to industry, pollution and how "deadly consumption only adds destruction".

This growing popularity was documented in the documentary *Beat This: A Hip Hop History*, and in Tim Westwood's film *Bad Meaning Good* later in 1987, showcasing young rappers like London Posse's Sipho and Bionic spitting bars in the back of a young Westwood's car on a drive around London. This period was significant in creating and cementing a unique identity for UK hip hop, and one that was not merely a carbon copy of anything State-side. Once rapping in your own accent became the norm – thanks largely to London Posse, believed to be the first to do so – crews and collectives began popping up all over the UK. There was a newfound respect for regional rap.

Names like Lancashire's Krispy 3, Glasgow's II Tone Committee and Bristol's Tricky are just some of those who emerged in the late '80s and '90s alongside London's Overlord X, Blak Twang, Ty and Roots Manuva. These male rappers and crews are a core part of UK hip hop history but, as Cookie Crew demonstrated, women were also always there, at the forefront; their presence was just diminished over time, or entirely erased. Numerous Black feminist scholars have written in detail about this erasure in the context of American hip hop, including Tricia Rose, Joan Morgan, Dream Hampton, Patricia Hill Collins, Imani Perry and Gwendolyn Pough. Rose, in her seminal 1994 book *Black Noise* notes, "In the early stages, women's participation in rap was hindered by gender-related considerations," going on to quote New York rapper Ms. Melodie: "It wasn't that the male started rap, the male was just the first to be put on wax."[2]

Monie Love, who became Queen Latifah's right-hand woman after her move to the States, was arguably the most successful UK export in the '80s, featuring on Latifah's feminist anthem and signature song 'Ladies First'. In addition to Love, women contributed significantly to shaping the culture in ways that went beyond surface level, especially in response to their position as women of colour in a largely patriarchal society. As hip hop grew as a commercial entity in the UK though, so too did a 'one in, one out' mentality, still often seen in the music industry when it comes to both gender and ethnic minorities. As the commercial value of hip hop as a marketable and profit-making endeavour increased, the role of women in hip hop generally shifted to something more cynical, which in many cases gave their contributions the appearance of being trivial.

"Women in hip hop, specifically, have battled against their marginalization since the genre's inception," states Janell Hobson and R. Dianne Bartlow in 'Introduction: Representin': Women, Hip-Hop, and Popular Music'. "However, their inclusion in this male-dominated music culture has drastically shifted in the mainstream reception of hip hop from their identities as emcees and deejays, who could hold their own against their male counterparts, to their relegation to hyper-sexualized roles as music video dancers, models, and groupies."[3] Relegation is the key word here. It is vital when considering how hip hop culture responded to women as the popularity, money-making potential and materialistic elements of the genre flourished. Shifted into purposefully more passive positions, women were relegated in ways that removed their agency and power as artists.

Journalist Vie Marshall was on the frontline in those early days the UK scene, working as a writer and rap columnist for around a dozen publications, including *Hip Hop*

Connection – the longest running monthly magazine dedicated entirely to hip hop culture. *HHC* was "one of the most eminent rap monthlies in the world, and as a result, the catalyst for a whole new sub-industry of UK hip hop magazines," said HUCK. "Magazines like *HHC* were instrumental in the careers of pretty much every rapper from the UK for a time, and in turn, paved the way for a new generation of MC."[4] The magazine existed from 1988 to 2009 and, in that time, helped document the incredible levels of innovation happening in the genre in all corners of the country.

"There were lots of other publications writing about Black music like *Blues and Soul*, *Record Mirror* and *Mixmag*," Vie begins, on her initiation into music journalism. "These magazines were covering some aspects of rap but [*Hip Hop Connection*] gave a lot of people a sense of community. Even if people were arguing, there was a forum that everybody had that they'd never had before. They also had this interesting thing where readers would write in to ask for a pen pal. You had lots of people connecting with each other that way, swapping tapes, swapping ideas, writing to one another."

It was a special publication and Vie was one of the magazine's stand-out writers documenting this thriving scene – refusing to let this relegation of talent occur. "I was the same age as a lot of the rappers that I would go and see," she explains, "so it just seemed that we had a lot more to talk about. As hip hop was burgeoning, so were we into our adult lives."

Vie admits that it took a while for the rappers she was meeting to truly embrace their identity and their Britishness, but when they finally did, it catalysed growth and progression unlike anything they'd seen before. "A lot of the British artists were trying to imitate Americans. Every now and then when I went over to America, I'd take over some British 12" records and cassette tapes and try to play them to these rappers and their management and get them signed or to do some collaborations. I think I did it about two or three times and then I had to give up because the Americans thought the British were a joke.

"The Americans were pretty territorial about their boroughs and things like East Coast, West Coast. They didn't want to hear anything coming from Britain. If they didn't want to hear something from the next borough, why would they want to hear something from another country? There were a few that did well though, like Monie Love. But I think it took off properly when the artists just didn't give a shit about sucking up to the Americans anymore and were using their own voices and their own experiences."

Hip Hop Connection was crucial in their support and encouragement of the scene but when it comes to writing about UK hip hop, and specifically women in UK hip hop, Vie was a distinctly important voice. In the

1990 article 'Ladies First', she wrote about "today's intelligent and articulate female rappers" who had "helped to remodel the traditional hip hop stereotypes of women". She speaks to Monie Love, Sandra from Wee Papa Girl Rappers, Donna from She Rockers, Betty Boo and others about sexism, media pressure and ambition, closing with a quote from Cookie Crew's Susie Q: "Women have already proved they can make rap music, and all that's left to say is that we'll be around for a very long time."[5]

Correct in her statement, so too was Vie in her demand for the contribution of women to be properly acknowledged – she was and remains a trailblazer for this dedicated emphasis on women's contributions towards making the scene innovative and exceptional.

"If you ask any random person who's a rap fan to name their top 10 or top 20," she says, "people will automatically reel off men. Even though there are lots of women who spit great bars, there's still a lot of machismo and a lot of condescension to females. The mid to late '90s were terrible for that."

Vie doesn't belong in the hip hop history books solely for her acclaimed work as a music writer, but also for taking a notable stand against sexism via the creation of Muthaland. Together with a group of fellow female journalists and DJs, Vie founded one of the very first hip hop club nights in the country. Its mission statement was to provide a safe space for hip hop expression and networking, with the Muthaland 'Muthas' at the helm channelling their feminine energy to grow the scene and open doors for others.

"The goal was to nourish this scene," Vie explains. "We had a couple of meetings, various people got wind of it and pretty much everybody seemed to want to be part of it. Our flyers said non-sexist, non-racist, non-violent and we had a policy that there would be no misogynistic lyrics played." There was a rule about avoiding records containing words like 'bitch' or 'ho' in them, although, as Vie reflects, those songs still found a way through in some unavoidable situations.

"London Posse came on and did a gig and the first thing they did was a song that they'd written just that week called 'Shut the Fuck Up Bitch You Can't Sing' which is apparently a dis for Betty Boo who was in She Rockers. The lyrics just kept on saying it for a good 16 bars and it went on and on. I just stood there thinking, *Are they thinking the piss?* But in the end, they said that they weren't going to charge us for their performance. Of course, I still had to get back on stage after their perform-ance to thank them! In a video that recently resurfaced you can see me pulling the microphone away from Bionic. To his credit, Bionic as he was coming off did say, 'Sorry Vie, I'm a bit drunk!'"

With many unforgettable anecdotes, Muthaland is a renowned part of the UK hip hop story and an early example of a safe space policy used at a club night. But it was more than just a fun night out for the community: the open mic competition was an exceptionally important feature for the wider emerging scene too. "It was a place for people who like hip hop and hip hop culture and where we could have an open mic so that we could discover the next generation or people that want to break into the industry. We'd contact every single record company every time that we were doing a gig, management companies too, telling them to come and sign this person. Because a lot people were still living at home with their parents or on the dole, we'd do stuff like give up-and-coming rappers a stack of 12" records so they didn't have to go and buy them. For the first few gigs, we would give out food. It ended up with us getting sponsored by various trainer and microphone companies. So, for the winners of the rap battles, we'd be able to give them prizes. We gave various people their first ever microphone."

The sheer impact Muthaland had on the culture is difficult to adequately convey, but it is, without a doubt – and to use Vie's words – a thrilling showcase of just how women can nourish the scene. Both in terms of accessibility and supporting the wider eco-system, they were also paying it forward in action.

Over the years, Muthaland had regular visits from the likes of Hijack, Stereo MCs, Tim Westwood, Rock-

Steady Crew and more, but aside from the rappers of the day being in attendance, there would always be prospective DJs, breakdancers, beatboxers and other artists enjoying themselves in the crowd. These were people that would continue to push the scene further, eventually going on to start their own crews or nights. Sarah Love, who proudly claims the title of being the only female DJ ever nominated for a MOBO Award, and the first to have a nationally broadcast hip hop show, didn't get a chance to attend Muthaland herself, but the spirit of the club night is evident in her own story. Sarah, who worked at specialist hip hop record store Deal Real Records in the late '90s, was one of very few female DJs on the scene but quickly found her community thanks largely to the store. In *Fact Magazine*, English rapper and comedian Doc Brown speaks about his connection to Deal Real and its wider importance to London's hip hop scene, describing it as somewhere for people that genuinely loved the art form, with no racial or class divides.[6]

"That's where I really first became connected with the hip hop community," Sarah says. Along with some school friends, she went on to start her own monthly party in London called Kung Fu, which began as something very small and humble but grew into a legendary element of the country's hip hop story. "I really cut my teeth through being in the record shop and being a resident DJ at Kung Fu, and the reputation I built there opened the door to many other opportunities as an international performer and broadcaster. 20 years later, I'm still managing to operate as a professional DJ."

Speaking to anyone that attended Kung Fu nights garners a similar level of excitement and delight to those that loved Muthaland and everything it stood for. These nights, and many others that came before and after, were about uniting people, amplifying voices and spotlighting the very best new talent around. Once Kung Fu outgrew the smaller London venues and moved to Camden's Underworld, there would regularly be upwards of 500 people in attendance, many unable to get in despite their best attempts. You could always expect to see Sarah and Harry Love on the decks, compered by Mystro, plus fresh talent on the open mic and guests like Skinnyman, Roots Manuva, Ty, Task Force, Jehst and Gang Starr's Guru causing mosh pits left, right and centre with their rhymes.

"Ultimately it was the people that made it, and they even eclipse some of the most incredible performances that we had." Sarah notes on her memories of Kung Fu. "I remember every month, standing there watching whatever show was happening and the crowd reactions and just thinking: this is so special. I want to soak this moment up and remember it forever because I know that this is classic."

As one of few women with the title of resident DJ, Sarah was conscious of her position. "I'm a competitive person anyway," she explains, "and my aspiration was never to be a great female DJ; I wanted to be a great DJ and I wanted to tear it down and not look like a fool DJing after Shortee Blitz basically! But as a female DJ at the time, getting on stage at a sold-out venue, next to the highest calibre of artists with a mostly male audience, the scrutiny felt different as a woman. It was as though people were waiting for you to cock up so they could say, 'You see, that's what happens if you let a girl DJ.' But that kind of comment was never going to happen on my watch."

"I revelled in shattering prejudice," she continues. "I was always like: right, tonight I'm going to absolutely send you to bits. I revelled in getting to play unadulterated, unapologetic hardcore hip hop and some of my favourite records and not give a damn, because that's what you came to Kung Fu for."

The power of representation should never be underestimated, be it on-screen, in pop culture or in the wider media. Vie and Sarah are both examples of women who lay the groundwork in male dominated fields and provided a reference point for those that would follow. While representation remains a significant talking point in contemporary culture, and things have advanced, the issue is still visible in the music industry. Recent studies, including a 2020 survey by the Annenberg Inclusion Initiative at the University of Southern California, continue to highlight the core drivers of gender inequality in the industry. Looking at Grammy nominations and songs of the Billboard Hot 100 Year-End Charts from 2012 to 2019 as evidence – the top female songwriter (Nicki Minaj) had 19 credits, compared to the top male songwriter (Max Martin) who had 43. Andrea Bossi notes in *Forbes*, "To improve the industry for women, survey respondents advocate for creating more opportunity; seeing more female representation and leadership; providing more support, recognition and resources; and tackling sexual harassment, objectification and ageism."[7]

The fact that a rapper has come out on top in this survey as far as women's songwriter credits go is a noteworthy milestone for hip hop, but the disparity between the male and female numbers in general is stark. There are masses of talented songwriters, performers, producers and DJs in hip hop today that are women – but what happened in the '90s, in the era between Cookie Crew and Sarah Love, that created what seems from the outside like a mass exodus? To answer that, we return to the 'one in, one out' mentality.

"When you actually take it back to the early days of hip hop," Sarah says, "there were lots of women involved in crafting this art. Women who were respected and were influencing some of the biggest and soon-to-be most influential dudes in hip hop's history. I think hip hop's expansion got to a point where the industry began to have a say over our culture and what was going to be given a budget and promoted to the mainstream. The music industry is pretty racist and misogynistic. The narrative that is commonly perpetuated of hip hop being fundamentally sexist – well, from my understanding, that's not how our pioneers started the movement. What mattered to our pioneers was not gender but being yourself and being fresh. So then we have to think, *Okay so where did that false narrative begin?* That began much later with artists who had corporate budgets behind them and marketing."

As more money was involved, objectification and sexism became the norm and more attention was placed on women's bodies and their potential as marketable objects, as opposed to just their skills. Tricia Rose observes this in *The Hip Hop Wars,* discussing the pressures imposed on women to play the roles of "bitches and hoes" in American hip hop: "Parallel to the elevation of the thug/gangsta figure is Black women's sexual self-exploitation for male viewing pleasure as a near requirement for female visibility in the male-dominated world of hip hop."[8] This wasn't how it began in UK hip hop; women were held on equal platforms to their male peers in terms of talent and skill. "Maybe I just wasn't paying enough attention to nonsense or maybe I just didn't give a damn," says Sarah, on avoiding the confines of sexist mentalities. "I was just fixated on showing the crowd and my peers alike that I'm very good at what I do and making anyone feel silly for even allowing any underestimation of me to cross their mind. I'm going to make you be afraid to DJ after me."

Vie agrees that women tend to be placed lower on the totem pole of hip hop in terms of respect and have been since the '90s despite their obvious contributions, but her feelings on this are again representative of a lot of the attitudes that make hip hop such a stellar space for women today. "Unfortunately, because the so-called mainstream will continue to see us as an afterthought," she says, "it's like fuck the patriarchy. Let's do our own thing. Don't be down with them, let them be down with you. They'll soon come."

And come they did.

Chapter 3:

The women who changed the game

"Why does it always have to do with my gender?" commented Little Simz in a 2016 *Vice* interview. "Why can't I just do what I want to do freely without feeling like people are trying to put me in a box all the time? Do you know how annoying that is? When you feel like you're doing something greater than life, but you're always just a female rapper?"[1]

Simz makes a very valid point, and one that has been percolating in my own mind since embarking on this project. Why focus on gender when gender doesn't specifically have any bearing on an individual's talent? It's a point raised by numerous interviewees too, with many stating their preference to simply be referred to as a 'rapper' as opposed to a 'female rapper'. In my day-to-day, I too make no obvious distinction when discussing genres of music; it's 'band' not 'female band', 'DJ' rather than 'female DJ' and 'singer' but never 'songstress'. My definition of woman is trans inclusive so I would always be wary of making any gender-based assumptions. However, it's a disparity that exists so widely in the music industry and has resulted in less pay, less respect and less credit for women and gender minorities over the years. In terms of talent, gender isn't relevant – in terms of treatment, visible legacy and structural issues, it is.

Women in CTRL's 2020 'A Seat at the Table' report reinforces why this conversation cannot be minimised. The report, which "analyses the makeup of team, board members, Chairperson and CEO positions across twelve UK music industry trade bodies" highlights that only 27% of CEOs across eleven music trade body boards and that 34% of board members across twelve music trade body boards are women. The report is even more brutal when considering women of colour; 0% of CEOs across eleven music trade body boards are Black women.[2] While this report focuses on roles behind the scenes, such an imbalance filters down. In this sphere, commercially successful women are seen as a rarity and so, only one woman or group can generally be equipped with full support and creative attention at a time. In an article for PRS for Music's *M Magazine*, hip hop artist and lecturer

Isatta Sheriff explains how this mentality is what leads to a distancing from the 'female rapper' label:

"The issue becomes even more evident when looking at shorter career spans of women, who often have to endure homogenisation from the media in which they are only acknowledged as part of a group and are overlooked as individuals. As a result, many choose to distance themselves from the 'female link up' categorisation; appearing in an all-women editorial features, or one off 'all female' collaborations, as the depiction often fails to reflect their creative reality."[3]

When we speak, Isatta clarifies why she believes it's still important to spotlight women, even though there is that hesitation in being defined by gender. "The toxic traits are still there," she says. "I think things have moved on, in some ways, but we still have that fight against patriarchy and misogyny and sexism. Some small battles have been won and now women are visibly making their own choices. I see a place for discussing it and there needs to be a place to highlight things that are not highlighted. I'm not against gathering and talking about girls just like I'm not against people highlighting Black History achievements because I know that the world is whitewashed."

Isatta began her career in the early 2000s under the name Tor Cesay, when UK hip hop and its various offshoots including grime were beginning to fully seep into public consciousness, thanks in part to the work of pirate radio stations like Juice FM and Mission FM. Isatta herself started out on pirate radio and says that it was normal at that time for girls to be involved. She didn't encounter much hostility until later, when it came time to advance her career, but she admits that there were some wounded egos and some friction from men who were afraid of being outshined by the girls.

"Whatever goes on within the industry is worse when it comes to Black music," she continues, "and then even worse when it comes to Black women. It is reflective of the whole industry. Certainly I felt more patronised and it wasn't that I wasn't feeling let in but I wasn't being given the time creatively."

Isatta, a talented producer and lyricist, is the founder of Doctored Sound, an independent record label and consultancy agency that delivers music education programmes and workshops for all ages. With her experience in the industry at the turn of the millennium, Isatta is candid about the capitalist influence on the genre and how she noticed this manifesting in the early noughties.

"The relationship between capitalism and hip hop is so strong that you can't separate yourself from it," she says. "When you look at the history of the recording industry, you can see how hip hop was literally put into the machine. From the beginning, it's been a commodity of the record industry and commercialised because of what sells, what's appealing or what people want."

In the UK, this is perhaps best exemplified when looking at the massive success of pirate radio, and how this was in time co-opted for mainstream audiences. Richard Bramwell makes an excellent point about this in his writing around the 2002 launch of BBC Radio 1Xtra: "Indeed, the British Broadcasting Corporation's launch of Radio 1Xtra, with a remit to play 'the best in contemporary Black music,' can be seen as a direct response to the success of pirate radio in meeting the needs of an audience that, at the turn of the century, the BBC was not."[4] The popularity of 1Xtra, which recruited DJs from local pirate radio stations, and the launch of other platforms like the cable TV station Channel U, signalled where hip hop and grime were headed and how the mainstream media capitalised on this enthusiasm. This was a particularly fruitful period for women in the genre too, with voices like Wildflower, Estelle, Tempa, The Floacist, Baby Blue, Shystie and Lady Sovereign emerging from the underground and finding success.

Ms. Dynamite, who was popular on pirate radio, released her debut album *A Little Deeper* in 2002, and went on to win the prestigious Mercury Music Prize. She became the first solo Black female artist and the youngest ever to win the prize, marking that the genre was being taken seriously by industry gatekeepers. Simon Frith, chairman of the judges of the Mercury

Music Prize, said: "It is a new kind of voice we hadn't heard before. Ms. Dynamite has a clear vision of what she wants to be. She can do it without being drawn into the cliches of the music industry."[5] Dynamite represented something vastly different – a mainstream return in the UK to the Cookie Crew-era of defiant and skilfully articulated lyrics and of speaking your truth over and above anything that could be deemed superficial. 'Afraid 2 Fly' addresses the "cold, cold world of war", while 'Brother' is an emotional ode to her younger sibling (Akala), who appears on the album's rousing finale 'Get Up Stand Up'. It was an indication of how rappers in the UK were maintaining that distinctive Britishness, attempting to break down sexist stereotypes that were so prevalent abroad. Against an industry pushing that sex sells, rappers like Dynamite came in without compromising vision or truth towards corporate demands, and stole the show in the process.

Muneera Pilgrim of hip hop duo Poetic Pilgrimage stresses how proud she is of British rappers. In all the iterations of rap in the UK, the common denominator has always been a genuine love of the music; as Dynamite's Mercury Prize win showed, talent and skill were prized first and foremost.

"I think that we have done something different," she says. "Just thinking about the rappers that we have in

Britain, and particularly thinking about the rappers going back, there's a certain consciousness that comes with it, generally speaking. I'm not saying everyone, but a lot of rappers were talking about where they were from and their realities. British hip hop didn't really have access to that much wealth at that time. If you're a girl, and you're playing on your womanhood, I don't think it's a bad thing. I think if it's empowering for that person, it is empowering for that person. What is important is balance all around and what I liked about hip hop growing up is that you had this full spectrum. Even if they weren't saying something specifically conscious, we understood the context of it. Whereas I think with rappers like Lil' Kim, we couldn't understand her world; her world was so far from ours that it just was not possible."

Muneera remembers the first time she heard A Tribe Called Quest's 'Check the Rhime' on the radio, which led her down the rabbit hole of hip hop. It was a genre that spoke to her heart but, being in Bristol, it was also clear that this was music that could speak to different communities and could be used to soundtrack what was going on in her immediate surroundings. "I remember in Bristol, we had this incident [in 1994] where a young Black man by the name of Marlon Thomas was attacked," Muneera says. "In fact, he lost his life and someone resuscitated him, and it was a racially motivated attack. That was the first time I felt moved to write my own lyrics."

Throughout the history of hip hop, rappers have been naturally drawn to the poetry of the genre to respond to issues like systemic racism and police brutality. When Rodney King was murdered by LAPD officers in 1991, Ice Cube, Tupac Shakur, Dr. Dre and others notably referenced the tragedy in their music. Likewise, hip hop is regularly described as the soundtrack to Black Lives Matter thanks to more recent releases by Kendrick Lamar, Common, Killer Mike and many more. In the UK, Marlon Thomas was dubbed "Bristol's Stephen Lawrence" because of the proximity between the cases – 18-year-old Stephen was murdered in 1993, while 18-year-old Marlon was beaten and revived with life-threatening injuries a year later. Muneera, in writing down her emotions as lyrics, was following in the long tradition in hip hop of expressing feelings while touching the community around you, especially those in need of something to communicate the pain. It was a lightbulb moment that made her appreciate what her voice and words could do, both for herself and for those around her.

After a move to London for university, Muneera and Sukina Pilgrim founded Poetic Pilgrimage in 2002. Though they initially operated on the poetry scene, the pair soon found their voice and community within hip hop at the new Deal Real Records store, which had moved from Soho to Carnaby Street. University friends Vincent Olutayo, Olu Olutayo, Sef Khama and

Tony Tagoe came together through a mutual love of the genre's culture and created what became known as "London's Hip Hop Mecca". Significantly, they had no specific connection to crews, or history linked to certain segments of UK hip hop – they just loved the music and wanted to create a hub of activity for up-and-coming talent, where new collaborations, networks and friendships could be forged.

"I give so much love to Deal Real in Carnaby Street because, they saw us, they liked us, and they accepted us for who we were," Muneera explains.

In contrast to the Noel Street store, in which more established rappers gathered, the Carnaby Street Deal Real "became a place of nurturing," notes Bramwell, "allowing aspiring young rappers to participate in this community."[6] It became a focal point in the early noughties for rappers around the country who would travel to participate in the popular open mics. Deal Real also sustained an international outlook, stocking music from European rappers, hosting international guests and making connections between artists the world over. For groups like Poetic Pilgrimage, this was important in their personal development, particularly once they had converted to Islam in 2005 and began to face extra hurdles as Muslim women in hip hop.

"I remember going to events that I used to go to before, wearing the hijab and people were like, oh, you're

Muslim now," says Muneera. "There was a distance. We definitely experienced a lot of Islamophobia; it was not cool to be a Muslim woman. No one took you seriously. Also, we had our own struggles with questions like *What do we wear, how do we dress? How do we embrace the new faith?* We realised that we had to define ourselves by ourselves. What this allowed us to do was to create a different genre of music or a different iteration of a genre that added our own influences into hip hop. We became a part of the world hip hop scene. Forget England for a moment, forget America for a moment; we were on tracks with Senegalese rappers, we were going on hip hop tours with global artists, going to South by Southwest. This allowed us to experience the world."

Poetic Pilgrimage are a crucial element of the wider UK hip hop story, both as part of the era of women rejecting the pressures placed on sexuality in the genre, and as Muslim women breaking down the barriers that stated women in hijab didn't belong in those spaces. "I am British hip hop, but a complication of what British hip hop is," Muneera notes. "Once you put on the hijab, sometimes in a space where it isn't familiar, it can confuse people." Poetic Pilgrimage changed these attitudes with their very presence in hip hop, but that wasn't always easy in post-7/7 Britain, as the 2005 terrorist bombings in London had created a new hostility around Islam.

In contrast, the duo's experiences in the US as Muslim women was bolstered by the strong bond that already existed between hip hop and Islam. A number of pioneers of American hip hop, like Big Daddy Kane and Rakim, identified as Muslim and followed the teachings of the Five-Percent Nation, which was a Black movement influenced by Islam founded in 1964 in Harlem. In the '90s, acts like Public Enemy and Mos Def openly referenced and praised the work of the Nation of Islam and their leader Louis Farrakhan in their music.

"Whenever we went to America, people were so respectful," Muneera reflects. "I remember it was the reunion tour of Hi-Tek and Talib Kweli. We were there at the back and then someone was like, it's the Muslim sisters, let them through! Not because they knew us but because they saw us with hijab. People respected the hijab, particularly in Black American communities."

People in their immediate circle back home were very respectful too, but it unfortunately took some time for the wider music industry to fully recognise their contributions. They were, however, admired for their honest and engaging live performances and thought-provoking content. Songs like 'Land Far Away', a remake of a famous reggae track by The Abyssinians pays homage to their Jamaican roots while referencing their faith, and 'Silence is Consent' is a bold critique of Muslim countries that are either silent about oppression, or who actually facilitate oppression against their own people. Poetic Pilgrimage were game changers, and for this and much more, their existence and influence deserves to be amplified. Across the hip hop spectrum, we see women facing obstacles and pressures on who or what they are expected to be – Muneera and Sukina were not only refusing to be forced into one singular image of what hip hop could be, but they were thriving while doing so.

Rachel Prager's career as Baby Blue was taking off around the same time that Poetic Pilgrimage were finding their feet in London, but Rachel's hip hop journey started as a teenager in the early '00s. She first caught the scene's attention with a track called 'I Woulda', inspired by her cousin's murder in the US. "That was the first song I ever put out," she says. "And I just went and dropped it off in DJs' pigeonholes at the radio station. From here, Rachel went on to work with fellow British rapper Estelle, who invited her to appear on 'Hey Girl' with John Legend and 'Don't Talk'; two tracks on Estelle's 2004 debut album *The 18th Day*.

Looking back, Rachel notes that the scene was definitely growing and evolving in commercial and mainstream popularity, but for women in hip hop "there had always been this feeling that only one gets supported at once. I think with female rap, it always takes longer because women always have to prove themselves 10 times more than men do sadly. I did feel that as a woman, especially as a young girl, I was pulled in a lot of different directions. I was given a lot of advice on how to behave, how to dress and how to look. That eventually made me just not want to be an artist anymore – I felt like a bit of a product or an object."

"When I look back at my own experience," she continues, "I would say, I wish I had just known who I was, stuck to my guns, not been led by it being a very male world. You get a lot of men telling you what to do, and how to act and what kind of music to make. I just wish that I just stuck to my guns and just been able to tune that out."

Rachel is now Head of Music at 7Wallace, Idris Elba's record label, so is in the unique position of working with and overseeing artists that are potentially experiencing similar types of hurdles and adventures, years later. "The way we approach our relationship with artists is very open, and I'd never try and get them to do something that they weren't comfortable with. I'd never expect them to compromise who they are for an opportunity. My career as a rapper has definitely shaped the way I am in my work now because I know how it feels when people are just trying to pressure you into doing something that doesn't feel good for you."

Women like Rachel are a vital piece of the music industry's eco-system and an example of the kind of individuals we desperately need to improve gender parity across the board. "There's definitely not enough of us," Rachel says, "and definitely not in leadership roles. I've worked with big record labels where I've felt like a minority, both being female and being a woman of colour. It just felt like there was only a few people that I could really relate to. We need more women in leadership roles. Especially for young women, you do need that guidance.

"You need to see that there are other women looking out for you that have got your back."

"There's a sort of rawness to it," says Rachel, on what made UK hip hop so noteworthy. It's the same thing that makes it remarkable today. "When you go to America, they always say, I love what you guys do. I mean, they're always complaining that they can't understand what we're saying. But they can recognise it as something special and different from the hip hop that comes out of the States. It's just raw and gritty and real, and that's what I love about it."

Rapper and musician Speech Debelle has similar feelings, pointing to experience as a distinguishing factor. "It definitely has a distinct quality," she contends. "We have a particular type of cadence, which is why things like grime just work so well for us. Our cadence is sharp, we don't draw out our words in a way that

North Americans do. Also, what's particular to us is the Caribbean scene. That's a different experience because somebody born Black Caribbean or Black Ghanaian, growing up in London is not going to be the same as somebody who has those identifiers but grew up in New York."

Speech won the 2009 Mercury Prize for her debut album *Speech Therapy*, becoming the first rapper since Dizzee Rascal in 2003 to pick up the award. Upon her victory, she was praised for both her storytelling and her natural lilt, with judges calling her a "remarkable new voice in British hip hop, tough, warm and reflective", adding, "She's just quietly telling her stories in the most beguiling way."[7] Like Dynamite before her, Speech took cues from the women who were rapping, spitting bars and making their presence known in those early days. In *Speech Therapy*, she covers frank themes like her own period of homelessness ('Searching'), her relationship with her absent father ('Daddy's Little Girl') and the pain of heartbreak ('Go Then, Bye'). Author and African American and Caribbean literature specialist Claudia May, in her assessment of Speech's skills, argues, "She neither treats rap purely as a brand of entertainment nor underestimates its capacity to provide individuals with opportunities to articulate their convictions."[8]

Like Rachel, Speech found hip hop as a teen, realising that she had a natural affinity for the rhythm and flow of rap while in secondary school. "My earliest memory of actually rapping was on the back of the bus," she explains. "The boys were rapping and my friends were like, 'She can rap too!' At that time, it was still very much the 'Girls can't rap' era. I did a rhyme and the whole top of the bus exploded. I remember that and I remember the feeling. I remember how surprised and shocked I was that it would have that reaction on people. I thought, *Okay, so there's something about this. There's something about when I use my voice, it cuts through.* Once I discovered rap and discovered that I didn't have to sing, it was all over for me."

Speech's Mercury Prize win in 2009 came as a surprise to some, with the rapper originally given among the lowest odds (8/1). Amy Granzin in her *Pitchfork* review of the album encapsulated why the wider hip hop community (beyond the UK) may hesitate to consider *Speech Therapy* a canonical record for the genre: "Debelle doesn't so much map 'street' as girl-next-door or Speech-from-the-block. Wherever she's from, anyway, some hip hop fans will likely write her off because the usual American rap signifiers – samples, seething synths, bombastic beats, and buckets of braggadocio – play scant part in her artistic agenda."[9] But *Speech Therapy* is a lyrically and musically exciting record; one that is structured with jazz and classical beauty in mind while also being conversational, challenging and emotive in its delivery. It feels fresh, and yet follows in the new millennium tradition of female MCs in Britain in its emphasis on poetry and lyricism above image and pageantry. It may have been underestimated for the Mercury because of relatively low sales before the award, but it's a cornerstone release in UK hip hop history. "It was a relief that I wasn't crazy," Speech remarks about her win. "I knew that I had come here for a reason; it's to do certain things. That was really important to me and it was just joyous."

"UK hip hop is a difficult game for females," said DJ Semtex, formerly of BBC Radio 1Xtra, in 2007. "But those who are serious about telling the world their message will be heard…The UK scene will never cease to surprise us. Just as we think it has hit a brick wall, a new star arises, or a new sound cuts through that changes the rules. We may not make a Missy Elliott, but we'll produce something totally different out of our own DNA."[10]

The 2000s showed how possible – and likely – it was for UK hip hop to follow its own distinct path, heading in a direction somewhat dissimilar to that of US hip hop. Professor of ethnomusicology Cheryl L. Keyes describes four distinct categories of women rappers that emerge in American rap performance: "Queen Mother" (the strong Black woman or maternal figure), "Fly Girl" (the lyrically talented but still cool and sexy woman), "Sista with Attitude" (the defiant woman who uses attitude as empowerment) and "Lesbian" (the woman that embraces her queer identity), using Queen Latifah, Salt-N-Pepa, Lil' Kim and Queen Pen respectively as examples.[11] In the UK, especially at the turn of century, women in hip hop amalgamated elements of each of these categories, in a way to avoid the binaries that the wider commercial hip hop scene subscribed to. To use and relocate Msia Kibona Clark's words within the context of the UK, "Women enter hip hop recognising the use of hip hop culture as an important space for creating one's own narratives and for challenging existing narratives."[12] As shown in just a handful from many possible pioneers to choose from, women in UK hip hop were creating and challenging, not merely following. As the critical success of rappers like Ms. Dynamite and Speech Debelle underscored, there was no defined formula. There was an openness to a range of styles and perspectives because of the nature of our rap DNA, feeding back to the road paved by rappers like Cookie Crew and those who came before. Female MCs might have been the minority in hip hop, but they have increasingly found new ways to move out from the shadows and into the spotlight – women in the UK were always innovating, experimenting and making their voices heard in unconventional ways, using their platforms to debunk and remodel new manifestations of their identity. They paved the way and changed the game for the next generation, out front and behind the scenes, and ultimately for the women who would come to rule hip hop today.

Chapter 4:

The women killing it across the regions

Genres ebb and flow in popularity. It usually happens in waves; a particular sound associated with a genre is adopted by a chart-topping artist, leading to commercial success. A tsunami of similar sounding hits follow, with that genre officially deemed 'trendy' and further pushed into the public sphere by music industry executives. According to new analysis from the BPI – the UK association of independent and major record labels – hip hop now "accounts for well over a fifth of all UK singles consumption – a six-fold increase on 1999."[1] Commercially, hip hop is in a healthy place in the UK and women are indeed a vital part of its success. Just like the genre itself, women in hip hop have had varying waves of popularity in the UK since the '90s, as artists and trends come in and out of fashion with new releases and new projects. To overlook women as part of the success and growth of hip hop however because of periods of fluctuation, as unfortunately many do in their various analyses, is to neglect an important piece of the puzzle.

By the mid-2000s, grime – the London-born, UK garage-influenced offshoot of hip hop – was taking real shape, with Dizzee Rascal, Wiley, Kano and others scoring big hits, followed by another surge in the 2010s featuring Skepta, Stormzy, AJ Tracey, Tempa T and more. Though a uniquely London genre in its inception, grime quickly spread to other parts of the country, primarily because of its emphasis on Black identity and localised experiences.

The emergence of grime scenes in other parts of the UK and this expression of similar lived urban experiences can be attributed massively to the rise of the use of social media in hip hop culture, with platforms like MySpace, Facebook, YouTube, Instagram and more recently, TikTok, giving artists opportunities without the need to necessarily travel to London. Not only has the internet allowed for a boom in regional hip hop and grime scenes, it has also been crucial for women in the genres, allowing them the freedom to write, release and share without permission or intervention from gatekeepers.

Isatta Sheriff has found the rise of digital media to be particularly useful in the more recent dissemination of her music. "As somebody who was in the mid-2000s generation of UK hip hop, people demand music from me and I'm putting out music this year but it is definitely due to the internet. I'm doing more of it now because it's not just one station who will play me when they think that you're hot. People of all ages enjoy music, they enjoy discovering new music and as much as I have lots of bad words to say about streaming, it has made people discover artists like me and legacy artists too."

Lady Leshurr is perhaps one of the best examples of contemporary rappers using social media as a means to share their work, embracing the generation predominantly using platforms like YouTube to find new music. In 2015, the Birmingham rapper had started releasing her *Queen's Speech* series of battle rap freestyles, the fourth of which led to a huge boom in popularity. It wasn't just her flow and lyrical talent though; Leshurr brought humour into her raps, fusing playful lyrics with the energy and high BPM of grime. Her viral *Queen's Speech* videos were each filmed in one continuous take, and at the time of writing, *Queen's Speech 4* has over 63 million views on YouTube. As she told the BBC in 2018, "YouTube has done everything for my career."[2] Her videos were watched around the world, not just in the UK, and the success of *Queen's Speech* led to her introduction to the American market. In a preview on her New York City debut, *The New Yorker* praised Leshurr, noting: "For years, British rap has reacted to the stylistic and cultural shifts of its American elders, but crossovers like Leshurr suggest that the Manhattan crowd may stand to gain from the Queen's English."[3]

Aside from giving rappers the chance to share their music globally, social media has also brought communities together, creating cross-country collaborations more readily. "Definitely, before a few years ago, it was just all about what was happening in London," Rachel Prager says. "Now you've got talent from all over the UK, which is amazing, because it shouldn't just be limited to certain areas. Now it's much more common for rappers from London, from Manchester and from Newcastle to collaborate. I don't feel like that was happening before; it would just seem like people would have to come to London to make themselves heard."

North London rapper Shay D has established her name within the underground UK hip hop scene, but social media has been a significant part of her journey, especially since she independently released her debut album *Human Writes* in 2018. "When I released my album and was planning to tour it," she says, "I was seeing that every time a lot of the guys around me in hip hop and in grime were doing an album release or a tour, they had their friends and other MCs open up their shows for them. They were bringing them out on stage, they had so many collaborations they were doing and I could see how much they were supporting each other musically, and how much it was helping their audience grow. And I looked at my peers, and other women in UK that were in rap and I couldn't really see anyone that was doing that. I didn't know if it was just because they didn't want to or because the labels or any of the gatekeepers didn't want there to be an element of competition. But I thought, *How has there not been a tour where all the women just come out and support each other and grow each other's audiences?"*

To celebrate the release of *Human Writes*, Shay decided to curate Queens of Art, the first ever all-female hip hop tour of the UK. The goal was to travel across the country to link up with local female rappers, celebrating sisterhood and standing up against misogyny in the process. She was able to connect with women – rappers, DJs, beatboxers and breakers – in other cities to bring her idea to life.

"I just really wanted to platform everyone and support everyone and mix our audiences. I sat there and cold called venues. I had promoters telling me it wouldn't work and people aren't interested in women in rap, and I had some promoters that loved the idea and were really supportive of it. On my socials, I was asking *Who raps in Nottingham?* Or *who's a female DJ in Birmingham?* People were contacting me all the time so I was researching, looking up everyone, DMing them – it was a lot of hours and a lot of work. But I just wanted to build a legacy and have an example that women can come out and unite, and it can widen our audience. Even my tour, I wouldn't have been able to connect with half of the women who I connected with if it weren't for social media."

Shay D's Queens of Art tour went up and down the country, taking in cities like Glasgow, Cardiff, Bristol and Birmingham, with incredible local women involved at each stop, including OneDa, Lady Sanity and SJ Soulist. "There are pockets around the UK where they are really doing their thing in their city, but I feel like other than on social media, it's quite hard to recognise if there's a buzz somewhere if you're not from there. So there are some people that think everything is very London-centric, and you need to come to London to make things happen. I think that's really, really changed and I think it's a really old school mentality. There is a lot of talent nationally."

When Shay D brought the tour to Glasgow, she was joined by a host of talented Scottish women, including Glasgow MC Empress, DJ and breaker Shelltoe Mel and future Scottish Album of the Year Award winner, Nova. Anyone lucky enough to be at that event in 2019 will speak highly of the sheer energy and force in the room, but as Shay notes, that camaraderie was present in every city because of the mutual support of all the women involved, and their desire to lift each other up. In separate conversations, Empress, Shelltoe Mel and Nova all praise the Queens of Art event as an example of what can be achieved when women come together in the genre. Each of them have had differing journeys in Scottish hip hop and though hip hop does have a long history and legacy in Scotland – going back to people like II Tone Committee, Krack Free Media and Blacka'nized in the '80s and '90s – as Empress and Mel confirm, there wasn't much attention given to women in the early days and even now, it can still feel like a boys' club.

"I first got into hip hop thanks to the 1987 Def Jam tour," Mel begins. "That was LL Cool J, Eric B & Rakim and Public Enemy at the Barras and I would have been around 15. The music just blew my mind but even before that, I had memories of watching a programme called *The Tube* which was Jools Holland and Paula Yates and they had Salt-N-Pepa on. They were the first women I had seen MCing and then it was people like Cookie Crew in the UK who I saw on Top of the Pops. Back then I was into the music but I also got into the dance from the Rock Steady Crew's videos, because they had B-boys and Baby Love was the first B-girl I saw. They had a big influence on me."

Mel found her niche dancing at clubs like Fury Murrys in Glasgow, where she was approached by someone who would turn out to be significant in her hip hop journey.

"This guy approached me who turned out to be Krash Slaughta [DJ Smiz] and he was in a band called Krack Free Media. I kept in contact with him and he used to send me tapes because there was no internet back then and I'd be practicing in my room. He introduced me to the 141 Posse and through them, I met many others. I ended up becoming the dancer for Krack Free Media and I remember dancing for them at an all-dayer at The Metropolis. Through that I met people like Big Div, Mistah Bohze and Defy. This would have been around the early '90s.

"Up here, back then there really weren't any female MCs, that I knew of anyway. There weren't any B-girls apart from Emma Ready who got into it around the same time as me. It's so nice to see nowadays that it's a totally different story, thanks partly to the internet. But back then you had to get your information from the videos. It could be very intimidating but I was lucky to have met Smiz and get in there. I do think that Scottish hip hop is still very much a boys club but it has been amazing to see people like Empress and others coming up over the years."

Like Mel, Empress doesn't remember seeing many other women in the scene when she first came to be a part of it. "We had Shelltoe Mel from the Flyin' Jalapeños Crew, there were other DJs and I remember MC Soom T. I think I was quite a solo warrior and it wasn't until

66

much later on that I saw women doing their thing which was fantastic."

Empress similarly found hip hop as a teen, getting properly immersed in the scene years later. "Big Div used to put on hip hop nights at a place called Hamishes in Paisley," She tells me. "Loki and people like that would be there but I didn't know who they were at that time. I was going through quite a difficult period to be honest; I was homeless twice before I was 17. A big part of the experience of being in the hostel was that you would naturally want to be anywhere but in those types of places. One of the places I found myself going to a lot was the studio. I ended up just hanging around, trying to get in with anyone I resonated with in that way. There used to be a group called Gaelforce, who used to rap in Gaelic and I would go down and watch them. I was only 16 at the time, but I used to sit and watch them making music. I think that's when I first got really involved with anything to do with Scottish hip hop."

After a break from hip hop, Empress was compelled to get back into it in the noughties, especially around the time of the Scottish Independence referendum. The poetry and defiance of hip hop lent itself quite naturally to this political period in Scotland, with many artists like Loki and Stanley Odd using art to debate and aptly express the frustration of so many Scots. Empress believes that more attention is generally being paid to regional hip hop, partly due to the way rap is used by artists to portray regional differences in terms of politics, culture and heritage, but also because of a sense of comfort in moving away from the London sound. "I think trying to be like a London rapper is something you maybe do when you're younger; you think you can try and maybe emulate the London sound. But with that being said, I think people are starting to take a lot more pride in their own regions."

There is bold and brilliant talent in Scottish hip hop, and while women like Empress and Shelltoe Mel have flown the flag for some time with their own community-based work, more effort is needed to encourage new generations of women MCs, DJs, breakers and more to get involved and take up space in the genre. Nova and her SAY Award win in 2020, is an excellent example, with her debut album *Re-Up* becoming the first hip hop/grime LP to win the national music prize. Aside from being a colossal personal achievement, Nova's win was significant for the genre itself in Scotland.

"The SAY Award has changed quite a lot of stuff for me and made me able to do what I want to do," Nova says. "But it's complicated as well because at first, it made me want to do everything and I realised that I can't take on everything at once. I had to strategize and think *Okay, I'll do things the way I would have done them before but hopefully it'll just be easier because I can just focus on work.*"

Nova's whirlwind year has involved plenty of press and live opportunities, but despite this, she agrees that the overall landscape is still a work-in-progress when it comes to accepting and praising women. "I think there are automatically more haters when you're a woman," she says, adding, "I don't think I'm taken that seriously. I'm taken seriously by some people but with others, I try to remind myself that they treat other people like that as well. It's kind of a symptom of not having a role model that's proven to you that you can be successful with music."

Role models are important – no matter our place in life, seeing those like us paving the way while holding the door open for those to follow creates untold opportunity. Shay D's Queens of Art tour proved women are willing and eager to boost each other, and with artists like Nova finding genuine success there is hope for future generations of women in hip hop. "There's definitely more respect and openness today because there are people that'll share things with you or try and get you involved," Mel summarises. "I think women are just getting on with it and doing it themselves like the Queens of Art tour. Surround yourself with people who feel you."

There is something special, to me at least, about Nova winning the Scottish Album of the Year Award and Deyah winning the Welsh Music Prize for *Care City* in the same year. One artist might have been an anomaly but two women in hip hop winning these national music prizes should be seen as significant in the wider UK scene; a sign of respect, value and pride in local talent. Like Nova, Deyah was surprised by her win but has since taken full advantage of the opportunities that have come her way, from appearances at major events around the country to the freedom to work on new projects. "I was the first mixed race or Black girl to win it," she says of the prize. "Over the past 10 years, a lot of winners had been Welsh folk, or pop or indie or alternative. 2020 was the first time a hip hop artist won. So that kind of just shows you that it's taken a while for hip hop to find its place in Wales. It has been very slow, but I would say there's more of a significant difference in terms of what the government are trying to do for music in a positive way, as opposed to how many more artists there are now compared to 10 years ago. I wouldn't say the scene has expanded much at all, but I do know in Wales, they're doing a hell of a lot to basically make the country a music hub."

Deyah wasn't aware of much happening in Welsh hip hop as a teenager, but once she discovered rap and her own abilities, she was determined to find her tribe and soak up any advice on getting fully immersed. Like so many regional artists before her, she looked to London for inspiration, which still happens quite naturally. "I do find that unfortunately, there were artists – including myself; I did this years ago – that would try and imitate what London were doing because London's success rate seemed higher than Wales. So you might listen to something in Wales and go, *Okay, the accent's definitely Welsh. But the beat and the lyrics are pretty much what you find in east London,* for example. However, when artists do hold on to the Welshness that they have – so they'll maybe include Welsh lyrics, even though they're rapping to a grime beat – I think that is nice in a way because it's like they still feel connected to Wales; it's not like they've completely turned into something typically London-sounding."

Proud of her Welsh identity, Deyah now feels that it makes her stand out, but also admits that she wasn't sure how impactful saying she was from Wales would be when starting out. "I did start to see myself lose part of my Welsh identity," she explains. "I just got wrapped up in the London scene, and I didn't really know if saying I was from Wales would benefit me. So, it's not like I'd say I'm from England, but I wouldn't be forthcoming in saying I was from Wales, until I kind of thought to myself, *No, you are Welsh and it's part of you, and you were born here.* There are loads of jokes in England that people have about the Welsh, and they don't really think that there's much going on here. It's just a land of grass with sheep and so that made me think, *I would like my next few years to demonstrate, or ultimately show, a bit of my culture, my Welsh side,* and I'd like to be able talk about Wales a bit more. I'm blessed to be able to have a platform where I can talk about Wales and actually put Wales on the map a little bit more."

The Welsh government has been active in its support of contemporary music, including hip hop, and such financial governmental support for culture can bolster the field, allowing for more creative freedom on the whole. To coincide with Welsh Language Music Day 2021, the government hosted Ysgol Hip Hop – a competition to get budding rappers at primary school level writing and performing. According to its website, "All you need to do is write and record a bilingual rap (using as much Welsh as you can) on the theme 'What the Welsh language means to you and your area'."[4] The competition was part of the government's policy ambitions to grow the Welsh language for future generations, done in a way that connects 21st century forms of vernacular with Welsh heritage.

"In a weird way, the reception from people being surprised that I'd won the Welsh Music Prize kind of made me think, *Oh, maybe we're not as far ahead as I thought we were,*" Deyah says. "But I've seen now, coming into 2021, that four artists that the Welsh Government is supporting are rappers. I think it's cool for the government to push hip hop; I think it's more the public who are trying to get used to it."

Having hip hop represented more widely on national stages is one way to normalise its inclusion in the arts more generally. Initiatives that bring under-represented artists together and encourage others to get involved are crucial in de-mystifying genres like hip hop for the public. In Cardiff, the creation of the music collective Ladies of Rage has been vastly beneficial in empowering women and non-binary artists to get involved with under-represented genres like hip hop, drum & bass, grime and dubstep. The collective now has over 400 members across Wales and provides a safe space to create and collaborate. Ladies of Rage member Amelia Unity is quoted in a BBC article, saying "I've always been into hip hop and I've always been used to being the only woman – or in the minority at least – at events. So I'm used to just being around men. After having been to a few Ladies of Rage jams and it being like this gap, that I didn't even know was a gap, was filled… I felt safe, where before I didn't even realise I didn't feel safe because it was just normal."[5]

Safe spaces are needed and can often do wonders when it comes to encouraging people traditionally on the outskirts to find their metaphorical home. It could be a collective or a group within the genre, as Queens of Art and Ladies of Rage show, but for some people of colour, hip hop has been that safe space, especially in locations where there may be few people of colour on the whole. Sara Santos, who goes by the stage name Don Chi, is an up-and-coming rapper based in Northern Ireland. She moved over from the Philippines when she was eight, and hip hop was one of her only ways of connecting to a non-white culture. "I do feel like that was my only connection," she explains. "Even though it was American, and it was mainly American hip hop I was listening to, those Black artists had a big influence on me. I did feel like I was a part of something. I felt like I was connected; like I wasn't alone."

Hip hop in Northern Ireland is growing thanks to people like Santos. "It's not really big over here, the whole hip hop thing, not that I know of anyway. I moved here when I was eight and I had to rewire everything; I had to relearn everything to be Northern Irish. It's so hard to explain my experience as a woman because it's hard for me to fit in as it is in the scene. I kind of get a bit over-whelmed by it all, because people will say, *She's foreign, she still doesn't know the culture*. So how do I tackle that as a foreigner and as a female?"

Santos exudes an air of confidence as she talks about her music. Her confidence comes from her wanting to be seen as an equal by the men in the scene, she explains, which isn't always easy. "I'm genuinely not doing this to tread on anybody's toes. I'm here to be like the lads. I want to be here with the lads not over the top of them. I don't know how many times I've been dissed by men, but I haven't reacted. I don't react because I don't care; I'm still going to be me. I'm still going to do what I'm doing. I'm still going to make music and it's not going to be affected by slander."

"It's just annoying, you know, because we're all in this together so there's no point in fighting," she continues. "But if they are going to fight with me lyrically, they're going to get crushed. I swear, one bar could ruin all of them. That's what they don't understand; it's like you know yourself that I have the power of the voice so why are you giving me ammo?"

This idea of 'being taken seriously' has arisen many times across my conversations. Nova spoke about it in relation to Scottish hip hop, but for many rappers in regional locations, there is an overwhelming feeling of being underestimated by those in London.

"People who have great content and great lyricism all throughout the UK are getting overlooked," Santos says. "The UK artists don't look at us as artists, because we don't have a scene to them. We're not big enough. Also, we're not a united Ireland, we're divided as people; that's why other people feel divided from us. There's a lot in Ireland but there's nothing in the North to help us succeed apart from the Oh Yeah Music Centre which is run by Gary Lightbody from Snow Patrol – so completely far from hip hop. How come we can't have our own platform? How come we can't have our mark on the map? But at the same time, I know it's because our own people aren't putting us on the map."

Just as hip hop became a beneficial tool for political campaigning in Scotland during the Independence Referendum, it's impossible not to question how politics in Northern Ireland may be connected to the local hip hop scene. It's risky to be rapping about politics – though respected by others in the scene when done right, says Santos, there has to be an air of caution. "It's a mixed community, the Irish scene; it's Protestant and Catholic. So going into politics and wording certain things about the environment that we're in, it's very hard. There have been some artists who have said certain things and have just never been seen in the scene ever again.

"I don't have a religion, I don't care about politics, I don't care about sectarianism but I'm cautious," she continues. "You get questioned about your religion and it's like, what the fuck does that matter to you? Is it going to change your life? Is it going to pay your bills to know whether I'm a Catholic or a Protestant? Are you going to stop listening to my music just because I'm either Protestant or Catholic? It can be as bad as that. And I think that's what's really stopping Irish hip hop from being pushed into the mainstream; because of the situation, because of the government, because of the politics. We can talk about certain things, but we can't at the same time."

In Ireland, hip hop is having a moment, with the popularity of rappers like Denise Chaila demonstrating the country's burgeoning talent. Northern Irish rappers have broken through, like Jun Tzu, Kneecap and Jordan Adetunji – who became the first ever hip hop act to play at the NI Music Prize in 2019; their success is a mere drop in the ocean of Irish hip hop talent. That women like Don Chi and others in her immediate vicinity haven't yet found similar levels of recognition is disappointing, but more so if it's down to the lack of industry support that exists for artists in Northern Ireland. Santos feels that the artists that do achieve some success beyond Northern Ireland in all genres could do more for their local scenes. "The bigger artists – not that they need to – but it would be nice if they would just give us a bit of recognition. Give us a bit of a step up by organising events online or organising things to help bring not just female artists but all artists together." It comes up time and time again – the scene thrives not when lifting up the ladder behind you; instead when holding it in place so that others can follow.

Rap is an expression of identity, and for as long as hip hop has existed, artists have used this poetry to communicate their unique and localised experiences. When it comes to rappers finding success and representing their own music scenes in the mainstream, there is evidence of a natural peak in interest for adjacent acts, and this is precisely why Don Chi is correct in her assertion that lifting each other up can be so worthwhile and why it's unfortunate that this isn't always standard practice. Rappers from regions within the UK – like Deyah, who proudly hypes up her Welsh identity – are able to shine a spotlight on the creativity of their locale. Women may not have been as visible in the early days of regional hip hop scenes outside of London, but as Empress, Shelltoe Mel, Nova, Deyah, Don Chi and Shay D and countless other women have demonstrated, the advent of social media and digital culture has revolutionised the way women are able to create, share and collaborate, removing the need to seek permission or approval. The destruction of this barrier has shifted the make-up of the industry, and who has the means to create and to share. We're now in a space that is defined by sisterhood and solidarity, where women work together and big each other up across borders, in a mutually beneficial way. The margins of hip hop have been broken down – women are taking charge at the front.

Chapter 5:

The women taking it into the future

Throughout all of the conversations for *Flip the Script*, there has been one unifying element: their willingness and enthusiasm to speak about the women they find inspirational in contemporary hip hop. While there is undoubtedly room for growth around inclusion in the genre, in the support of trans and non-binary artists for example, the positivity that radiates from each interviewee exemplifies the hope and general feelings of confidence that exist today. That the scene is thriving. That women are coming to rule hip hop.

What women have achieved in UK hip hop is extraordinary; what they continue to achieve with the advancement of digital culture and cross-border collaboration is nothing short of heartening. Joelah is an up-and-coming entertainment presenter, who hosts a weekly show on Rinse FM where she plays a mix of grime, hip hop and soul. "It's just out of control now," she tells me, "but in a really good way. As a DJ, and someone who is constantly looking for new music, there's so much out there. In terms of the digital space, it's opened up so many new opportunities, and not just for hip hop. For someone like me, for presenters, for content creators, for models, even. There's beauty in not looking like what they told us we were supposed to look like, growing up. I think it's the same with hip hop as well; there's beauty in all the differences. At the end of the day, it's poetry."

Joelah believes that the opportunities are in abundance thanks to digital culture. "If you can't find one, you can create your own," she says. "That's what people are doing right now, so I'm excited for it and I can't wait to see the next generation of rappers. I do this thing with Ruff Sqwad Arts Foundation, it's called Grime Pays, where we take a group of kids who are interested in doing something in the music industry, and we teach them how to make a beat and about the business side of it. I do a presenting workshop for their confidence and at the end of the week, they perform. Every year there have been more females coming in and doing it, and that just gives me so much hope."

"The wave of UK female artists that are coming through just feels really strong," says Rachel Prager. "The music is high quality and it feels like it's being heard. There's still a lot of work to do but I'm definitely optimistic." Similarly, Empress talked of her excitement for any woman who picks up the mic: "I know how hard it is when you're doubting yourself because you've got men in the room that might want you to be a certain way." She draws specific attention to the socially conscious yet trend-setting style of Shay D and Ms Banks as current favourites.

Other names to add to your must-listen list were Ivorian Doll (Nova: "She's got such a big personality and openly says that she raps about stuff that girls care about."), IAMDDB (Debbie Pryce: "When she delivered her first record, I just thought there was no one like her.") and Nolay (Susan Banfield: "I listened to something she did the other day and my jaw dropped. I said, *My gosh, this girl is unbelievable.* Just the flow, the freestyle, the lyrics – I actually couldn't believe what I was seeing.").

Prager listed Shaybo and Lavida Loca, and almost everyone brought up Little Simz at some point – unsurprising considering Simz is one of the finest talents we've ever seen in UK hip hop (a bold claim, perhaps, but I stand by it). There was, however, another name mentioned across the board – Enny. "I just think she's absolutely remarkable," Muneera of Poetic Pilgrimage said. "She's definitely my one to watch." Prager and Cookie Crew's Susan Banfield also had similar comments, the latter professing, "I think lyrically, she's just amazing." Both Simz and Enny are exceptional in how they use their poetry to interrogate themes like systemic racism, familial conflict and womanhood, all the while doing so with an introspection and hyper-personal viewpoint that feels both real and relatable.

I tell Enny this when we eventually catch up and she's visibly flattered to have fellow rappers – and pioneers in the genre, at that – pick her out as their one to watch. The south east London rapper and singer is a fast-rising star, her 2020 breakout hit 'Peng Black Girls' not only putting her on the radar, but sending her viral on TikTok after Jorja Smith jumped on the track's remix. It's a mellow and uplifting celebration of Black women and individuality, refreshing in its positivity, standing in contrast to the commonly heard braggadocio of much of modern hip hop. "Weirdly enough, one of the reasons I was hesitant to really pursue music," Enny says of her lyrical and thematic focus, "was because I always thought that no one would really care what I had to say. I'm not going to show my boobs, I'm not rapping about sex so is there really a space for that? To be where I am at the moment and to now be in a place where people are interested in the kind of stuff I'm talking about is an honour and a privilege."

Enny has been drawn to hip hop since childhood, but actively starting recording and posting freestyles on YouTube from around 2018. Her brand of hip hop is reminiscent of the consciousness and feminist energy of game changers like Queen Latifah, Monie Love and Cookie Crew, but her soulfulness and lyrical prowess also recalls the likes of Lauryn Hill. When asked about who she personally looks up to, she names north London rapper Lex Amor. "Her artistry is mad and [2020 album] *Government Tropicana* is such a beautiful project," she says. "It's a different dimension of rapping. That's the cool part about female rappers today; there are so many dimensions they can come from. You can be woke, you can be sexy, you can be hood, you can be street – there are so many lanes to be across."

In contemporary hip hop, there are so many different lanes that women traverse so dressing 'sexy' and being socially conscious is much more customary and accepted than it perhaps was at the turn of the century. Not only that, the emphasis on and normalisation of women's sexual freedom by rappers like Nicki Minaj, Cardi B and Megan Thee Stallion is seen as a form of feminist protest against the hyper-masculine and patriarchal rule of hip hop. As American historian and academic Robin Kelly argues, "The introduction of new discourses can, and has, proven an important influence on the politics of rap music. Not only have Black women rappers played a crucial role in reshaping the attitudes toward women among a substantial segment of the hip hop community, they are also largely responsible for raising the issue of sexism within rap."[1] Hobson and Bartlow reiterate this in their analysis of women's contributions to feminist discourses in hip hop: "Despite mainstream hip hop's increasingly commercial and misogynistic focus, and with fewer opportunities for women in popular hip hop to create or sustain politically conscious music, there is nonetheless an intrinsic relationship between hip hop and feminism."[2]

Enny agrees that we're in an interesting and fruitful period and is proud to be a part of that. "I feel that women are doing great and that there's a nice renaissance moment that is happening right now; there's a very strong wave of female artists. I'm privileged to even be in conversations and just even be in the room with so much talent." Like so many others, Enny does feel awkward about the gendered label, though she's hopeful it will dissipate. "I find it annoying that it always has to be female rappers," she says, "because the talent is just rapping and it's like just because I'm a woman doesn't mean I'm not better than another rapper. I feel like a lot of the women right now are better than the male rappers. So, people might say, 'She's a sick female rapper,' but it's like no, she's a sick rapper regardless of her gender. You're always going to be seen as a female rapper but I feel like maybe having more women in these spaces will take away from that and it will just be what it is."

"I feel like there's been an expansion," she continues, on the surge of hip hop communities across the country. "We're getting an insight into hearing different British accents in music, and I think that's pretty cool because it does bring a whole other dimension and allows more inclusivity. London is great, but the UK is bigger than London, and there's so many more stories to tell. Hip hop is about storytelling; I feel like that's the beauty of it."

There are so many talented women in hip hop in the UK today, and this will only accelerate. If we have not already surpassed the tipping point, then we are right on its precipice. "I also think that we're in a whole different world, and the industry isn't as in control as it used to be," Enny adds. "You have a direct connection to your audience, all you have to do is pick up your phone and push your content and it can reach anyone. So I feel like that also has created a freedom, because a lot of people don't need to sign; the labels aren't now always picking who they want. The people are picking and the labels are catching on after."

"It's definitely going in a positive direction because we've got many high profile females here who are getting serious attention and acknowledgement, even in the mainstream," picks up Sarah Love. "And these women are being taken seriously as artists, as people whose careers are going somewhere."

"I think it's already happening," Speech Debelle notes. "We are much closer to understanding that feminine energy is a compass that we should be following. And that's how its moving. When I listen to my cousins who are younger, and hear how they're speaking about sexuality and the concepts and ideas that they have, I'm more than confident. I think the future of women in the industry and outside of it is better than it has been, ever.

"I think we're wild women and wild women are the women who change the world."

Conclusion:

The women to whom
I owe the world

As I type, Little Simz is preparing for the release of her fourth studio album, *Sometimes I Might Be Introvert*. Predictably, it's already being hyped as one of the potential albums of the year, even though only four tracks have been unveiled so far. 'Woman' has been the soundtrack to the later stages of *Flip the Script*, as Simz shouts out women from all over the world, while singer Cleo Sol provides a soaring, empowering hook. It's a tribute to the strength and beauty of women everywhere, and its lyrics and rich soundscape have been reverberating around my brain as a constant since its release. Perhaps because this book is my own tribute to women just like Little Simz and those that came before her.

Going into this process, I knew that I would find myself frustrated; both by the general lack of emphasis on women in hip hop literature, and by the accounts of the women interviewed, who deserve so much more praise for their contributions. Writing this book has proven to me what I had always known – women have been at the very heart of hip hop since its inception and are the future of the genre too, despite attempts to erase and diminish their work over the years. But it has also given me a whole new appreciation of hip hop in its power to articulate the experiences of predominantly Black youth, even in highly localised and regional settings away from major cities. The way hip hop has evolved from its roots in the Bronx to London, then regions like Manchester, Birmingham and the north of England, to Scotland, Wales, Northern Ireland and beyond highlights its power as an art form and as an expression of marginalised experience. I'm as fascinated by it as I am appreciative of its existence, and I'm excited to continually find new ways to immerse myself in all aspects of the culture.

As we emerge from a year of closures, cancellations and collective pauses in the music industry, there's plenty of talk of how we build back better so that more artists are supported and that the barriers to entry aren't so high. A major element of this is ensuring that women and marginalised genders, particularly those of colour, are encouraged and invited into traditionally male-dominated spaces in the music industry so that the entire landscape can evolve. I've waxed lyrical about why I think women are the future of hip hop in the UK, but there is undoubtedly still work needed by the wider industry, not only in backing female talent but also in taking hip hop more seriously as a major UK genre and cultural behemoth. I asked everyone I spoke to in *Flip the Script* about what they felt needed to change to move the genre further and, also, to encourage and support more female MCs. Here's a snippet of what was said, and perhaps a manifesto of action for the future of a thriving scene:

1. Give young women a more significant radio platform – radio play is still a big income stream for artists
2. More spaces for women to work uninterrupted, and funding and support to facilitate this so they can invest in their own skills
3. Managers and labels – truly get behind the women they represent so they feel adequately championed
4. More community spaces and access to recording studios for women, perhaps financially supported by radio stations and labels
5. Be intentional about bringing women into the fold; create safe spaces for one another

6. Encourage young people to study music business. The more that have good ideas and experience, the more they could potentially help other emerging artists
7. More collaboration and less competition – when women work together, there is a proven impact and power in their output. It's about getting together and helping each other out, not tearing anyone down
8. More women are needed in gatekeeping roles and behind the scenes – trustees, chairs of boards, DJs on national radio, videographers, and more
9. Recognise that there's not one way to be a woman. There are so many different representations out there, and people not being represented – it's time to bring the voices to the table
10. Push and believe in what women have to say in these spaces and set an example with not only words, but actions too
11. Hold the door open for each other

There is no magic wand solution that will fix all of the music industry's woes when it comes to representation, misogyny and historical toxicity, but as the lights once again come on, now is the time to take action, instead of merely speaking about it. That means putting real time, money and resources into championing under-represented voices in genres like hip hop, who are at the forefront in terms of their talent and innovation.

I've always felt connected to hip hop – to its defiance, its raw emotion and its poetry. But it is to the women, particularly the Black women, who have battled stereotypes and gendered social expectations that I owe the most. To Queen Latifah and Monie Love for being those women on the TV that I respected way back when; to Cookie Crew for always leading by example at home and abroad; to Ms. Dynamite and Speech Debelle for doing their own thing and proving the naysayers wrong; and to Little Simz for carrying the torch with such soul-baring grace, talent and extraordinary swagger.

Flip the Script is my tribute to those who have crafted the safe haven to which I visit often, and a safe haven to which I hope you may venture into too. This is my tribute to them and to the women who are still to take up their space in the genre. To those women, I say remember the pioneers but take the sceptre and own your voice. It is the most powerful tool of all.

References

Chapter 1:
The women who built the scene

1. Clover Hope, *The Motherlode: 100+ Women Who Made Hip-Hop* (New York: Abrams Image, 2021), 4.
2. Kathy Iandoli, *God Save the Queens: The Essential History of Women in Hip-Hop* (New York: Dey Street Books, 2019), 44.
3. Hope, 4

Chapter 2:
The women who spread the word

1. Andy Wood, "'Original London Style': London Posse and the Birth of British Hip Hop." *Atlantic Studies*, vol. 6, no. 2 (Aug. 2009), 176.
2. Rose, *Black Noise*, 154.
3. Hobson and Bartlow, 3
4. Eric Thorp, "How Hip Hop Magazines Shaped UK Rap as We Know It." *Huck Magazine* (31 Oct. 2019).
5. Vie Marshall, "Ladies First." *Hip Hop Connection* (1990), 30-34.
6. Tam Gunn, "An Oral History of Legendary Record Store Deal Real." *Fact Magazine* (4 Apr. 2015).
7. Andrea Bossi, "These Are 3 Of The Biggest Drivers Of Gender Inequality In Music." *Forbes* (26 Mar. 2021).
8. Rose, *The Hip Hop Wars*, 235.

Chapter 3
The women who changed the game

1. Sam Wolfson, "Little Simz Is Going to Change British History, One Step at a Time." *Vice* (3 Aug. 2016).
2. Women in CTRL, "A Seat At The Table." (Jul. 2020).
3. Isatta Sheriff, "Women in UK Hip-Hop." *M Magazine* (11 Mar. 2021).
4. Richard Bramwell, "Council estate of mind: the British rap tradition and London's hip-hop scene." *The Cambridge Companion to Hip-Hop* (Cambridge University Press, 2015), 261.
5. Angelique Chrisafis, "Ms Dynamite's victory blasts Mercury norms." *The Guardian* (18 Sep. 2002).
6. Bramwell, 259.
7. Rosie Swash, "Speech Debelle wins Mercury music prize." *The Guardian* (9 Sep. 2009).
8. Claudia May, "'NOTHING POWERFUL LIKE WORDS SPOKEN': Black British 'Femcees' and the Sampling of Hip-Hop as a Theoretical Trope." *Cultural Studies*, vol. 27, no. 4 (July 2013)
9. Amy Granzin, "Speech Debelle: Speech Therapy." *Pitchfork* (6 Aug. 2009).
10. Hattie Collins, "'We can beatbox just as well as the boys.'" *The Guardian* (1 Nov. 2007).
11. Cheryl L. Keyes, "Empowering Self, Making Choices, Creating Spaces: Black Female Identity via Rap Music Performance." *The Journal of American Folklore*, Vol. 113, No. 449 (Summer, 2000), 256
12. Msia Kibona Clark, "Feminisms in African Hip Hop." *Meridians*, vol. 17, no. 2 (Nov. 2018), 384.

Chapter 4
The women killing it across the regions

1. BPI, "Rap and Hip Hop soars in 2020 fuelled by streaming, new BPI insights show." (15 Apr. 2021).
2. Steven McIntosh, "Lady Leshurr: How tooth brushing made a YouTube star." *BBC News* (11 Apr. 2018).
3. Matthew Trammell, "Lady Leshurr Comes to New York." *The New Yorker* (3 Dec. 2015).
4. Welsh Government / Llywodraeth Cymru, "Get involved in a battle of the beats and rhymes on Welsh Language Music Day." *Gov.wales* (2020).
5. Catherine Evans, "Ladies of Rage: Musicians find a 'safe space' in sisterhood." *BBC News* (8 Mar. 2021).

Chapter 5:
The women taking it to the future

1. Robin D. G. Kelley, "Kickin' Reality, Kickin' Ballistics: Gangsta Rap and Post-industrial Los Angeles." *Droppin' Science: Critical Essays on Rap Music and Hip Hop Culture* (Philadelphia: Temple University Press, 1996), 146.
2. Janell Hobson and R. Dianne Bartlow, "Introduction: Representin': Women, Hip-Hop, and Popular Music." *Meridians: Feminism, Race, Transnationalism*, vol. 8, no. 1 (Oct. 2007), 4.

Further reading

For a full reading list to further dive into the subject, visit 404ink.com/flipthescript.

Acknowledgements

First of all, I'd like to thank Heather McDaid and Laura Jones for believing in me enough to commission this book as a part of their awesome series. I wouldn't be anywhere if it weren't for their faith, expertise and encouragement all the way through (and even well before) and for smacking down that imposter syndrome when it reared its ugly head!

Thanks also to Dave Hook for sharing his wisdom and immense hip hop knowledge, and to Lekan Latinwo of Intricate Management for making so many vital introductions for me.

This year has been difficult for so many people for so many reasons, but on the work side of things, I wouldn't have made it through without the professional advice of people like Nikki Simpson and James Hewes, and without the epic support system created by my List girls

– Deborah Chu, Becki Crossley and Megan Forsyth. I owe so much to Kirstyn Smith, Halina Rifai and Francesca Sobande for their unbelievable friendship and their constant reassurance. It has been and continues to be invaluable.

Thanks to my family, especially for 'The Tape', without which this book probably wouldn't exist. Also, to all the women who were kind enough to lend their time for interviews during this process, to all the incredible hip hop scholars out there whose books I adore and to all the women who I didn't get a chance to mention (there are so many; check out the playlist!). And to you for reading and engaging with this book; it means the world.

Finally and most importantly, to Adam for being my partner and best friend, and to Begbie for being Begbie.

About the Author

Arusa Qureshi is a writer and editor with a particular focus on music, diversity and accessibility within arts and culture. She was formerly the Editor of UK entertainment and events guide *The List*, and her work has appeared in *Bella Caledonia*, *gal-dem*, *the Guardian*, *GoldFlakePaint* and more. Twitter: @arusaqureshi

About the Inklings series

This book is part of 404 Ink's Inkling series which presents big ideas in pocket-sized books.
They are all available at 404ink.com/shop

If you enjoyed this book, you may also enjoy these titles in the series:

Love That Journey For Me: The Queer Revolution of *Schitt's Creek* – Emily Garside

Love That Journey For Me dives deep into the cultural sensation of Canadian comedy-drama *Schitt's Creek*. Considering the fusion of existing sitcom traditions, references and tropes, this Inkling analyses the nuance of the show and its surrounding cultural and societal impact as a queer revolution.

On His Royal Badness: The Life and Legacy of Prince's Fasion – Casci Ritchie

On His Royal Badness examines how Prince's distinctive style both on and beyond the screen disrupts hegemonic, hetero-normative and Black masculinities and contemporary fashion more generally. Taking core pieces from his wardrobe, Ritchie embarks on a wide-ranging exploration of how the simplest of pieces can tell the most incredible of stories.

The End: Surviving the World Through Fictional Disasters – Katie Goh

The End studies apocalypse fiction and its role in how we manage, manifest and imagine social, eco-nomic and political disaster and crises. What do apocalypse narra-tives tell us about how we imag-ine our place in history? Why do we fantasise about the end of the world? What does this all unveil about our contemporary anxieties?